Blanche Saunders:

DOG CARE

AND

TRAINING

FOR BOYS AND GIRLS

Drawings by Haris Petie

NEW EDITION
1982—Third Printing

HOWELL BOOK HOUSE, 230 PARK AVENUE

NEW YORK, N.Y. / 10169

BOOK ONE

DOG CARE
for Boys and Girls

TO BOYS AND GIRLS

This book is really two books in one.

Previously published separately, they have now been combined to give you a more complete and more convenient guide—and help you make your pet the "best" dog in town.

BOOK ONE—DOG CARE FOR BOYS AND GIRLS tells you how to feed, groom and bathe your dog. There are tips on how to keep your dog healthy; what to do in an emergency; how to recognize parasites. You will learn about dog shows, obedience and field trials. You will discover many things about dogs that you never knew before.

BOOK TWO—DOG TRAINING FOR BOYS AND GIRLS shows you how you can train your dog to be a good friend, a winner of the C. D. (Companion Dog) Obedience degree, or even a trick dog. You love your dog. If you teach him good manners, your parents and friends and neighbors will love him, too.

CONTENTS for BOOK ONE
DOG CARE FOR BOYS AND GIRLS

If your puppy could talk, he would probably say, "This has been an exciting day." He might even add, "I'm rather sleepy. Think I'll take a nap." When your puppy doesn't want to play, don't force him. Puppies are like babies—they sleep more than they stay awake.

If your puppy didn't eat the dinner you so carefully prepared, blame it on the toys you bought him or on his inquisitive nature. Adventure and curiosity are a part of every puppy's make-up.

[7]

You found a tooth on the floor? That could very well be!
Puppies change teeth, just like people. The baby tooth you
found made room for a permanent one.

And that wart on his face was there when you bought the
puppy. You just didn't notice it in your excitement of getting
a new playmate.

The small swelling on your puppy's tummy (if there is a swelling) is called a hernia, probably caused at birth. If it doesn't disappear, ask your veterinarian about it later.

Perhaps you are wondering where the puppy will sleep! Why not put him in the bathroom with papers on the floor. A playpen or a wire cage would be even better. If you tie the puppy, use a leather collar, a chain leash and *don't* leave him alone.

After your puppy has been in his new home fifteen or twenty minutes, take him outside for exercise. This will teach him to stay clean in the house.

And in case he is thirsty, give him a drink of water.

Puppies puddle without warning. They cry when you leave them. They chew. They bring up their dinner from excitement. Be patient! Don't give in to the puppy and don't become annoyed, and before long you will think he has lived with you always!

Never call your dog and then spank him. When he does something wrong, go to him. Hold him by the collar; then scold or give him a shaking.

Don't *yell* at your dog. The right tone is more effective. Besides, dogs don't like to be yelled at.

Never *chase* your dog to catch him. Kneel; then coax him to come by tapping the floor or the ground.

Never *grab* for your dog. Reach for him slowly, and pick him up gently.

Avoid games where your dog nips in play. Biting can become serious.

Be consistent! If it is wrong one time, it is wrong another.

Never *pull* things from your dog. Tell him, "Out!" Pry his jaws apart, then pat him after he lets go.

Never *tease*. Play in a nice way.

And when your dog has been good, give him a reward.

THINGS TO REMEMBER

Dogs get hungry as people do. Feed your puppy at regular hours, and give him a well-balanced diet. Mother can advise you on this.

Give him fresh clean water and exercise daily. In summer, change his water *twice* a day.

B z-z-z-z

In fly season, spray your dog or keep him indoors. Flies annoy dogs as well as people.

Teach your puppy while he is young to stay alone so he won't bark and chew when you leave him. A wire cage is the safest place.

Give him a bone, but only the shin or knuckle variety that won't splinter. Or you can give him a strip of rawhide which can be bought at a pet shop.

Don't leave your dog without shade in summer.

Don't make him sleep where it is cold or damp.

Roll up the car windows when you take him riding. When your dog must be left in a parked car, have the car parked in the shade and open the windows slightly so he can't jump out and so he cannot suffocate.

If you tie your dog to a stake, don't leave his leash dangling; he could choke on it.

Don't use a collar that will slip too easily over your dog's head.

Above all, *train* your dog to obey you. Other people will like him better, and it will help keep him safe.

FEEDING YOUR DOG

When a puppy is small, dinnertime comes often, unless you use the self-feeding method and food is kept before the puppy all the time. Here are some general rules for feeding:

3 months or under	3 to 4 times a day
3 to 6 months	2 to 3 times a day
6 months to 1 year	1 to 2 times a day
1 year and over	Once a day.

This is a good schedule for the young puppy:

8 or 9 A.M.	Milk and cereal.
Noon	Meat and cereal with extras.
4 to 5 P.M.	Same as at 8 A.M.
7 to 8 P.M.	Same as at noon.

When your puppy goes on three meals a day, feed him milk in the morning. Give a solid meal at noon and again during the early evening. When he goes on two meals a day, feed milk in the morning and the solid meal during the late afternoon.

WHAT'S FOR DINNER?

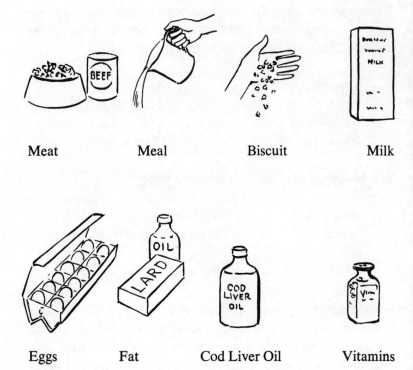

Meat   Meal   Biscuit   Milk

Eggs   Fat   Cod Liver Oil   Vitamins

Dicalcium Phosphate

Meat can be fed raw or cooked. It can be ground up or in chunks, or it can come from a can. Select the kind of meat your dog likes but don't give him pork.

Meal and biscuit can be fed dry or they can be moistened with hot water. Most dog meals are a complete dog food and all you have to do is add fat.

Milk is fed to young puppies because they need the calcium, but if your older dog likes milk, it won't hurt him.

Give one egg two or three times a week, but cook it or feed just the yolk. Raw egg white contains albumen, and this is not good for dogs.

Cod liver oil is important in winter. In summer, sunshine supplies the vitamin D that every dog must have.

Your choice of fats include lard, butter, cooking oils, bacon drippings or fatty trimmings.

Dicalcium phosphate builds strong bones and helps quiet nerves.

A one-a-day vitamin pill should fill your dog's vitamin needs.

HOW MUCH?

Is your dog:

Very small?   Small?   Medium?   Large?   Very large?
The amount of food needed will vary according to your dog's size:

Meat  to

⅛–¼ lb   2–3 pounds

Meal or
Biscuit to

½–1 handful   Several cupsful

Extras to

½ Teaspoonful   2 tablespoonsful

Ask the person from whom you bought your dog how much food to give him, both as a puppy and as a grown dog.

FEEDING TIPS

As your puppy grows, so must the amount of food you give him. Feel your dog's body. Do his ribs and hip bones stick out? If so, increase his dinner! If his bones are hard to find, cut down a little. A healthy dog should be in good weight, neither too fat nor too thin.

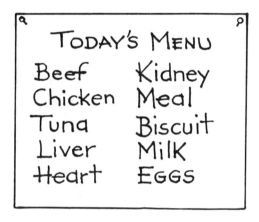

TODAY'S MENU

Dogs thrive on an unvaried diet, but if you want to give your dog a change, feed cooked oatmeal, cooked rice, cottage cheese, cooked beef hearts, liver, tripe or mutton. Feed cooked fish and chicken, but be sure there are no bones.

A dog should clean his plate within a few minutes. If your dog leaves some of his dinner, try feeding him two meals a day of smaller amounts. Perhaps he will like it better.

Canned dog food comes in the form of pure meat or in the form of a "ration." The meat should be mixed with meal or biscuit or some other cereal, such as cooked oatmeal or shredded wheat. The ration is a complete dog food by itself.

If milk gives your dog diarrhea, substitute chicken or beef broth.

You may not like fat but your dog will, and he should have fat.

One "fast" day a week (like going without candy) will help your dog have a good appetite. This means going without food entirely, *including tid-bits.*

When a dog eats such things as sticks, stones, dirt or animal droppings, something may be lacking in his diet, or it can be a more serious trouble sign. If your dog craves the unusual, consult your veterinarian because the dog may have something wrong organically.

Feed your puppy at regular hours. Feed your older dog at the family's convenience, but not from the table.

Water? Keep it available at all times, unless your dog is sick or you are having house-breaking problems and water is being limited.

Ice water in hot weather, is something your dog will appreciate anywhere at any time. Carry a thermos with you in the car during the summer.

As a final reminder, don't forget your dog's cracker or biscuit at bedtime. Dogs like to eat before going to sleep too.

Keep the water dish from being tipped over.

Keep the water pan cool and free of dust and insects.

So, your dog has short hair! Groom him twice a week anyway. Use a damp sponge and wipe the dust from his coat. Brush him with a stiff brush or use a grooming mitt that slips over your hand. A hack-saw blade will help to remove dead hair.

For long-haired breeds, you need a brush, a long-toothed comb and a carder. Break the mats apart with your fingers, then comb to the skin. Cutting the mats leaves the coat uneven.

You may need help, but when you groom your dog, take care of other important things. Otherwise, it is like washing your face and leaving a dirty neck.

[26]

Clean his eyes with a piece of cotton dipped in warm water. Caked eyelids cause sores.

Pull out what hair you can from his ears, using your thumb and first finger. If the ears are dirty, clean them by wrapping a piece of cotton around your finger then dipping it in alcohol. B.F.I. powder (you can get this at the drugstore) is a good antiseptic. Use it to prevent ear trouble.

Snip off the pointed ends of the toenails with a nail cutter. Use a file to shorten them even more. Be careful not to make the nails bleed.

Tartar, the dark brown substance on the teeth, can be taken off with a scaler, the kind your dentist uses. To keep your dog's teeth clean and his gums healthy, rub them once or twice a week with tooth paste or cotton dipped in Milk of Magnesia.

Does your dog have a bad breath? Wash his teeth and gums with ALKALOL (not alcohol). He will smell much sweeter.

Shorten the hair under the tail of your long-haired breed so he won't have trouble going to the bathroom. Otherwise he might get sick or have painful sores.

Cut away wads of matted hair or chewing gum from between the dog's paws. Remember what it felt like when you had to walk on stubble or had a stone in your shoe?

Grooming your dog is not only fun; it is a privilege. Start by using the right tools. Someone who specializes in your breed can tell you what brushes and combs to buy.

Have a regular place to do the grooming. Your dog will then know what to expect.

Stand your dog (unless he is a very large dog) on a steady work-bench or table. Help him feel secure.

Make him behave. If he struggles, hold him firmly until he stops struggling, then brush and comb him again.

During the grooming, check for skin trouble. Skin trouble is caused by an allergic reaction to insect bites, food, faulty diets, external irritants, fungus and bacterial infections, and many other causes. When you notice the least bit of skin irritation, take your dog to the veterinarian immediately. If you don't, the dog might be in for real trouble.

If your dog scratches, look for fleas, lice or ticks. If he is free from parasites, look for something the dog might be allergic to—his food, shampoo, or whatever you use to clean his sleeping quarters.

WORMS AND
HOW TO RECOGNIZE THEM

Not every dog has worms but *can* get them. Here are the most common:

Roundworms: You can recognize roundworms immediately. They are from two to five inches long, and they have a firm, round body, almost white in color.

Tapeworms: You won't see the whole tapeworm unless your dog was wormed for tapeworm and he passed one. Watch for segments. You will find these in the stool or on the hair under his tail. One-eighth to one-fourth inch long, pinkish-white when passed, they turn to a light brown when exposed to air. Tapeworm segments when dry remind one of little grains of rice.

It takes an expert to recognize *hookworms* and *whipworms*. They are no larger than a hair. For positive identification, your dog's stool must be examined under a microscope. Your veterinarian can do this.

Heartworms are not as common as the four we have mentioned, but they can be serious. The blood, instead of the stool, is tested. A dog with heartworm may have trouble breathing and he is usually very thin. Where the other worms live in the intestines, heartworms live in the heart, as the name implies.

Here are some things you can do to help keep your dog free of worms:

Have the dog's stool checked at regular intervals and worm him when necessary.

Disinfect and keep the dog's living quarters clean.

Use a spray to repel flies and mosquitoes. Dogs get worms from insects and animal droppings.

Get rid of fleas. This means a bath for your dog and a change of bedding.

If your dog is confined to a small outdoor run, pick up the stools daily. A toy rake and shovel will do the job just fine.

EXTERNAL PARASITES
AND HOW TO RECOGNIZE THEM

Fleas are brown and they move very fast. Look for them on your dog's head and stomach.

Lice are small, gray in color and difficult to see. They are usually found on the dog's ears and the sides of his face. Don't worry about dog lice getting on people. If they do, they never stay.

Ticks have four legs on each side of their body. Male ticks are brown and rather small. Female ticks are grayish tan, and when they are ready to lay eggs they are sometimes as big as a grape.

Use Pearson's Creolin in the bath water to rid your dog of fleas and lice. Don't make the solution too strong, and be careful of the eyes.

For a tick remedy, ask your veterinarian or local pet shop owner to recommend some product. An ordinary bath won't kill ticks.

In tick season, feel through your dog's coat every day. When you find a tick, hold it close to the head with a pair of tweezers and *shake* it loose. Destroy it; don't throw it away!

BATHING YOUR DOG

Every dog should have a bath when he gets dirty or if he has parasites. Take these precautions:

If your dog has long hair, comb him first. A matted coat never looks clean because you can't get the soap out.

Put cotton in his ears and a drop of castor oil or some vaseline in his eyes to protect them.

Have the water warm and no higher than the dog's elbows.

Use a rubber mat so he won't slip.

Use a mild shampoo so as not to irritate the skin or hurt the eyes. Nothing is better than pure castile soap. If your dog has fleas, add Pearson's Creolin to the bath water and wash around his neck first so the fleas can't run to his head. Be extra careful to protect the eyes.

Rinse the coat thoroughly to remove all soap.

After the bath, take the cotton from your dog's ears, dry him with a hair dryer or rub him briskly with towels in the hot sun.

Keep him warm for at least two hours, especially in winter.

BATHS MADE EASY

A flat, wiping sponge, like the one mother uses to wash the dishes, is just right for washing your dog's face. Buy one for your dog, and put his name on it. Use the sponge also to cover his eyes to protect them from soap.

Use a thick sponge to remove water from his coat before you towel him. Your dog will dry quicker and you won't need so many towels.

If your dog has long hair and you want him to shake, blow in his ear and duck. Otherwise you will get a showery bath.

Skunk? Pour a can of tomato juice over your dog after you bathe him, let it dry, and rinse the coat thoroughly. Tomato juice will take skunk odor off the dog but not off his leather collar.

To keep your dog healthy, have him examined by a veterinarian at regular intervals. Ask about distemper, hepatitis, leptospirosis and rabies shots. And don't forget the booster shot that every dog should have once a year.

Don't let your dog sniff strange dogs or where dogs have been.

Disinfect your dog's feeding dish and his water pan. Wash them in very hot water to which a detergent has been added.

[37]

If you have been near a sick dog, wash your hands and change your clothes before you go near your dog. Germs are easily carried from one place to another.

THE SICK DOG

This is how you will know if your dog is sick:

He will be more quiet than usual.

He will act droopy.

He may refuse to eat or will eat very little.

If he has a fever, he will feel hot when you touch the inside of his back legs.

His eyes will have a tired look.

Don't ignore *symptoms.*

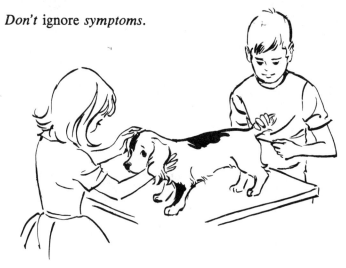

Ask someone to help you take your dog's temperature. Use a rectal thermometer. Shake down the mercury, dip the bulb end in vaseline or rub some soap on it, then insert it in the dog's anus. Let it stay for two minutes.

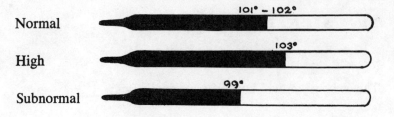

Normal   101° – 102°

High   103°

Subnormal   99°

If your dog's temperature is normal, the thermometer will read between 101 and 102 degrees. A temperature over 103 degrees or less than 100 degrees is equally dangerous.

TROUBLE SIGNS

You need help from your veterinarian if your dog:

has diarrhea repeatedly,
has a high temperature,
has a subnormal one, for long,
vomits repeatedly,
eats unusual things such as hair, wool, dirt or animal drop-
    pings,
drinks an abnormal amount of water,
urinates frequently,
passes blood in either the urine or the stool,
has convulsions.

RULES FOR THE SICK ROOM

Keep your dog warm.

Keep him quiet.

Keep him away from other dogs.

If he has diarrhea, take away solid foods. Give "honey water" (1 teaspoonful of honey to 1 cup of warm water) three times a day.

If the stool is white and chalky, this means your dog is constipated. Give a mild laxative such as Milk of Magnesia, one teaspoonful to two tablespoonsful, depending upon the size of the dog.

Take your dog's temperature morning and night.

Report a change in temperature to your veterinarian.

When you put your dog back on regular food, do it gradually. Feed such things as raw meat, meat broth, rice and dairy products.

Put liquid medicine into a small bottle. Back your large dog into a corner or straddle him. Hold the dog's head up. Pull out the lower lip at the side to form a pocket. Pour in a little medicine at a time, then rub his throat to make him swallow.

Support the small dog by kneeling.

When you give your dog a pill, hold the pill between your first and second finger or between your thumb and your first finger, and poke it down your dog's throat as far as you can. When you take your hand away, pull the tongue gently toward you, then release it. Hold the dog's mouth closed and rub his throat until he swallows.

An easier way is to wrap the pill in a piece of meat or if it is hard, crumble it in some ice cream. Some pills are gelatin outside with a liquid inside, and you should make sure your dog swallows them whole.

Epsom salts are good for a swollen paw. With hot water, but not hot enough to burn, soak the paw three times a day for at least ten minutes.

If your dog claws at his face, see if something is caught between his teeth or in the back of his mouth. It could be a wire or a piece of string, perhaps even a bone.

If your dog has been in a dog fight, go over him carefully. Wash all wounds with disinfectant and check them daily. Dog bites become infected easily.

The purpose of a splint is to keep a broken bone from becoming more damaged. If your dog should break his leg, keep him quiet and the leg rigid until the bone can be reset.

Hornets and bees sting dogs as well as people. A good home treatment is an ice pack or household ammonia. If the dog has been stung severely, take him to the veterinarian as quickly as you can.

We hope it doesn't happen to your dog, but if he should be hit by a car, throw a blanket over him and muzzle him before you move him. A dog in pain may bite his very best friend.

Dogs swallow many things they should not. A teaspoonful of salt on the back of his tongue will make your dog vomit such things as part of a sponge, small metal objects or spoiled food.

If your dog swallows a chicken or fish bone or some other sharp object, such as a pin, feed bread soaked in water or give him some mashed potatoes—as much as the dog will eat. If you can't get him to the veterinarian immediately, continue the home treatment every two hours.

If you ever have to bandage your dog's paw, don't make the bandage too tight. Keep the paw dry and check at intervals for signs of the leg swelling. Rubbing the bandage with soap, or alum or bitter apple from your drugstore, might keep the dog from chewing it.

An Elizabethan collar will keep your dog from scratching at a sore ear or a spot on his face. To make the collar, you need cardboard, a pair of scissors, a shoestring or a piece of twine. Cut two over-lapping half circles from the cardboard, with an opening the size of the dog's neck. Punch holes and tie them together with the string. Your dog will look funny, but don't laugh AT him; laugh WITH him.

Does your dog cry when he scratches his ear? The ear may be infected. An ear with a sour odor and smelling of wax, needs veterinarian treatment.

A dog will drool when is hungry, but a bad tooth will cause saliva to drip from his mouth.

A runny nose but no fever, may mean your dog has caught a cold. Give him one aspirin (¼ to ½ if he is a small dog), keep him warm and quiet and watch for other signs of sickness.

If he swallows with difficulty, look at your dog's throat. If it is red and inflamed, this could be serious. See the veterinarian!

A cold, wet nose is usually a sign of good health. A hot, dry nose may indicate a fever. It is not uncommon, though, for a dog to have a cold nose and still be very sick. Rely on your thermometer.

Your dog doesn't have to be near a sick dog to catch a disease. Germs are carried on our hands, our clothing, our shoes, by insects and by the very air we breathe. This is why you must be careful to wash your hands and change your clothes if you have been near a dog that is sick.

YOUR DOG'S MEDICINE CHEST

Rectal thermometer

Boric Acid Solution (for eyes)

Tincture of iodine or metaphen (for wounds)

Milk of Magnesia (as a laxative)

Kaopectate (for diarrhea)

Aspirin (as a sedative and to fight fever)

Yellow Oxide of Mercury—2% (for eye injury)

Petroleum jelly (for thermometer and use on skin)

Suppositories (to aid in housebreaking, traveling)

Zonite or some other disinfectant (antiseptic)

Pearson's Creolin (for fleas and lice)

B.F.I. powder (for the ears)

Epsom salts (for sprains or paw injuries)

Skin ointment (as recommended by your veterinarian)

Gauze bandage

Cotton

Adhesive

Even the most gentle dog will bite when he is in pain. Sometimes dogs bite when they are being groomed. If for any reason you have to muzzle your dog, use a strip of cloth, a piece of gauze bandage or an old silk stocking to tie his mouth shut. This is how to do it:

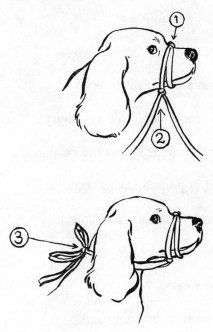

Tie a knot on the top of his nose, then one under his chin, and finally, make a bow-knot on the back of his neck. Make sure his lip is not caught between his teeth.

HOW TO LIFT YOUR DOG

Lift your dog by holding him close. Support his chest with one arm and let him sit on your other arm. It hurts when you pull your dog up by his front legs or lift him by the skin on his neck. You might even injure him.

HOW TO TIE YOUR DOG

When a dog is tied, he gets restless and pulls on the leash. To keep your dog from tightening his knot, tie him like this. Then all you have to do is to slip the free end through the loop and pull.

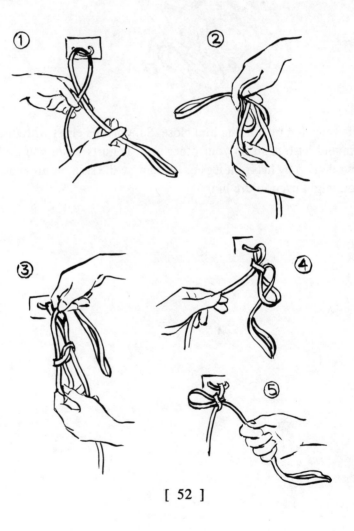

HOW TO WEIGH YOUR DOG

You can weigh a dog in one of three ways. Weigh the very small puppy in a basket on the kitchen scale. Turn the adjusting knob to zero with the basket in place. While the puppy is in the basket, hold your hands near him so he can't fall out.

If you can pick up your dog, step on the bathroom scale and see what you weigh together. Subtract your weight from the total and you will have your dog's weight, just like that.

If your dog is large, train him to sit and stay on a scale with a flat platform. Who wants to lift a Saint Bernard?

After your puppy is past the chewing stage, give him a basket, a blanket or a pillow to sleep on, and place it where there is no draft. If he sleeps out of doors, raise the bed off the floor or the ground to keep it free of dampness.

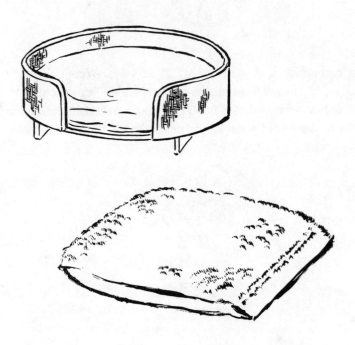

Cedar shavings or sawdust make a good outdoor bed for short-haired dogs or for those whose coat lies flat. For long-haired breeds, such as Poodles or Maltese, shred papers or cover a pillow with a towel that will launder easily.

SWEATER? RAINCOAT?

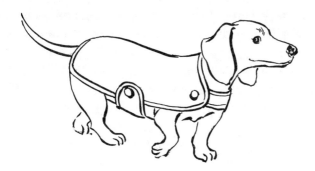

Animals that live outdoors in winter grow their own fur coats. House pets live in heated buildings and ride in warm cars. If your dog is low-slung like the Dachshund, or if he is one of the Toy breeds, a coat or a sweater will protect his tummy from snow and from rainy sidewalks. If you own a Poodle and take away nature's protection through clipping, he needs a coat to keep him warm.

CAR SICKNESS

There is no magic cure for car sickness, but these things might keep your dog from getting sick every time he goes in the car:

Take him riding while he is still a puppy.
Take him riding every day and on short trips.
Don't feed him before you take him riding.
Leave windows partly open for air.
In persistent cases, allow the dog to sit in a parked car.
Feed him in the car.

If he still gets sick, a sedative or a sea-sickness pill might help.

While riding, if you think your dog is going to get sick, hold his head UP, rub his throat and make him swallow.

Some people believe car sickness is caused by loss of balance. This centers in the ears. Cotton in the ears or covering them in some way may help.

THE FEMALE DOG

Don't be ashamed to use the word "bitch." This is the proper word for your female dog.

A bitch normally comes in "heat" or in "season" twice a year. This is the period when, if you breed her, she will have puppies.

A bitch's season lasts about three weeks. You will know when she comes in season because she will have a colored discharge.

If you don't want to raise a litter of puppies, keep her away from male dogs the full period of her season. If you breed her, keep her confined anyway.

It takes 63 days for a bitch to have puppies. Puppies are born blind. Their eyes open between ten days and two weeks.

DOG SHOWS

If you are wondering about dog shows, there are several kinds:

At an *All-Breed Show*, dogs are judged on their appearances.

At *Obedience Trials*, they are judged on how well they perform a series of working tests.

In *Field Trials*, sporting dogs are judged on what good hunters they are.

Specialty Shows are those in which only one breed is exhibited or only one event is held, such as an Obedience Trial.

For dog show purposes, all pure-bred dogs are divided into six Variety Groups:

SPORTING DOGS

Wirehaired Pointing Griffon	American Water Spaniel
Pointer	Brittany Spaniel
German Shorthaired Pointer	Clumber Spaniel
German Wirehaired Pointer	American Cocker Spaniel
Chesapeake Bay Retriever	English Cocker Spaniel
Curly-Coated Retriever	English Springer Spaniel
Flat-Coated Retriever	Field Spaniel
Golden Retriever	Irish Water Spaniel
Labrador Retriever	Sussex Spaniel
English Setter	Vizsla
Gordon Setter	Welsh Springer Spaniel
Irish Setter	Weimaraner

SPORTING breeds are used for hunting and retrieving birds.

HOUND DOGS

Afghan	American Foxhound
Basenji	English Foxhound
Basset	Greyhound
Beagle	Harrier
Black & Tan Coon-hound	Ibizan Hound
Bloodhound	Norwegian Elkhound
Borzoi	Otter Hound
Dachshund	Saluki
Scottish Deerhound	Whippet
	Irish Wolfhound

HOUND breeds track other animals.

WORKING DOGS

Akita
Alaskan Malamute
Australian Cattle Dog
Bearded Collie
Belgian Malinois
Belgian Sheepdog
Belgian Tervuren
Bernese Mountain Dog
Bouvier des Flandres
Boxer
Briard
Bullmastiff
Rough Collie
Smooth Collie
Doberman Pinscher
German Shepherd Dog
Great Dane

Great Pyrenees
Komondor
Kuvasz
Mastiff
Newfoundland
Old English Sheepdog
Puli
Rottweiler
Saint Bernard
Samoyed
Giant Schnauzer
Standard Schnauzer
Shetland Sheepdog
Siberian Husky
Cardigan Welsh Corgi
Pembroke Welsh Corgi

WORKING breeds were originally bred to perform special services such as herding sheep or acting as guard dogs.

TERRIERS

Airedale
American Staffordshire
Australian
Bedlington
Border
Bull Terrier (both Colored and White)
Cairn
Dandie Dinmont
Smooth Fox
Wire Fox
Irish

Kerry Blue
Lakeland
Manchester
Norfolk
Norwich
Miniature Schnauzer
Scottish
Sealyham
Skye
Soft-Coated Wheaten
Staffordshire
Welsh
West Highland White

TERRIER breeds are experts when it comes to catching animals that live under the ground.

TOY DOGS

Affenpinscher
Chihuahua (long coat)
Chihuahua (smooth coat)
English Toy Spaniel
  (Blenheim and Prince
  Charles)
English Toy Spaniel
  (King Charles and Ruby)
Brussels Griffon
Italian Greyhound
Japanese Spaniel

Maltese
Toy Manchester Terrier
Papillon
Pekingese
Miniature Pinscher
Pomeranian
Toy Poodle
Pug
Shih Tzu
Silky Terrier
Yorkshire Terrier

As you can tell from the name, TOY breeds are small dogs.

NON-SPORTING DOGS

Bichon Frise
Boston Terrier
Bulldog
Chow Chow
Dalmatian
French Bulldog

Keeshond
Lhasa Apsos
Miniature Poodle
Standard Poodle
Schipperke
Tibetan Terrier

Breeds that do not fall into a special classification are placed in the NON-SPORTING GROUP.

HOW A DOG BECOMES A
BREED CHAMPION

Dog show classes are divided into six classifications:

The Puppy Class

> The Puppy Class is for dogs under a year old.

The Novice Class

> The Novice Class is for dogs that have never won first prize except as a puppy.

The American-Bred Class

> Dogs entered in the American-Bred Class must be born in the United States.

The Bred-by-Exhibitor Class

> Dogs shown in the Bred-by-Exhibitor Class must be bred and owned by the person who handles the dog, or by a member of the family.

The Open Class

> The Open Class is open to all dogs and, except for puppies, dogs born in other countries must be shown in the Open Class.

The Winners Class

> The Winners Class is for those dogs that win first prize in the classes mentioned above.

The Puppy, Novice, American-Bred, Bred-by-Exhibitor, Open and Winners Classes are also divided by sex.

THE AMERICAN KENNEL CLUB
CHAMPIONSHIP CERTIFICATE

This certifies that

BETSWORTH JUDY VAN BUREN

ENGLISH SETTER   SA-142534

owned by _____ BETSWORTH KENNELS

having completed the requirements for a championship

on ___ JUNE 22, 1963 ___ *has been officially recorded a*

CHAMPION

by The American Kennel Club

P.B. Everett
Secretary

[63]

(*Dogs*)			(*Bitches*)		
Puppy			Puppy		
Novice			Novice		
American-Bred	}	*Winners Dog*	American-Bred	}	*Winners Bitch*
Bred-by Exhibitor			Bred-by-Exhibitor		
Open			Open		

The dog and bitch that take first prize in the Winners Class win points toward their championships. The number of points depends upon the number of dogs and bitches shown that day. The dog and bitch that win second prize in the Winners Class receive a ribbon that says *Reserve Winners*.

When a dog or bitch receives 15 championship points under at least three different judges, with two of the wins being major ones (three points or more), the dog becomes a champion of his breed. The word Champion or the letters CH. appear before the dog's name. He remains a champion for life.

The Winners Dog and the Winners Bitch, together with the dogs that are already champions, then compete for *Best of Breed* (or *Best of Variety,* if the breed has more than one size or one color.)

Following Best of Breed competition, the Winners Dog and Winners Bitch are judged against each other for the *Best of Winners* ribbon. (Of course, if either has won *Best of Breed,* he or she is automatically Best of Winners.) The Best of Winners is entitled to the highest number of championship points earned by either sex of the breed.

The final award is called *Best of Opposite Sex.* If a male wins *Best of Breed* or *Best of Variety,* a female is named *Best of Opposite Sex.* If a female wins, a male takes home the red and white *Best of Opposite Sex* ribbon.

HOW A DOG GETS INTO THE GROUP

All Best of Breed or Best of Variety winners are eligible to enter their variety group to compete against the other Best of Breed or Best of Variety winners in their group. There are four placings in each group and the ribbons are the same as in the classes: blue is first, red is second, yellow is third, and white is fourth.

A Best of Breed or Best of Variety winner is not required to enter his respective group, but if the dog enters and wins his group, he *must* compete for BEST DOG IN SHOW.

HOW A DOG IS NAMED
BEST IN SHOW

It is possible for a judge to select one breed of dog as being better than another breed by comparing each dog to the written standard for his breed. For example, the Chihuahua in the Toy Group is judged against the "perfect" Chihuahua; the Pomeranian in the same group is judged against the "perfect" Pomeranian. When the first place winners of the six Variety Groups compete against one another and the judge selects a single dog as Best In Show, in his opinion, that dog came closest to the standard for his breed on that day. The ribbon is a beautiful red, white and blue rosette.

BOXER

(Every breed has a standard of excellence.)

HEAD in correct relationship to skull; never too small; clean; with neither deep wrinkles nor dewlap; typical, unique

EYES dark brown; not too small nor protruding nor deep-set; expression of energy and intelligence; dark rims

STOP distinct but neither forced into forehead nor sloping; furrow between eyes

NOSE broad, black, slightly turned up somewhat higher than muzzle; nostrils broad

MUZZLE square, powerfully developed in length, breadth, depth; not pointed, narrow, short, shallow

JAWS wide: lower protrudes beyond upper; bends slightly upward; upper broad where attached to skull; undershot; bite powerful, sound

CHEEKS well-developed, no protrusion

MASK dark, confined to muzzle; in distinct contrast to head color; a REQUIRED trait

UPPER ARM long, forms right angle to shoulder blade

CHEST deep, reaching to elbows; depth, half of height at withers

FORELEGS straight, parallel; bones strong, firmly joined

FEET small, tightly arched toes (cat's paws); hard soles; turning neither in nor out

COAT short, shiny, smooth, tight to body

SIZE: Weight, males, at 23" height, weight over 66 lbs.; females at 22", weight 62 lbs. Height, males, 22"-24" at withers, not under; females, 21"-23" at withers, not over

BODY well-balanced; medium-sized; square in profile, sturdy, short; muscular, clean, powerfully developed; skin taut; equipped for speed, never racy

LIPS upper, thick, padded; lower edge rests on front of upper lip; lower must be perceptible viewed from front; teeth, tongue must not show when mouth is closed

TEETH sound, powerful bite; lower incisors in straight line; upper, slightly rounded; middle incisors do not project. This creates frontal width in both jaws, canine teeth widely separated. Upper corner incisors fit snugly back of lowers

SKULL top slightly arched; occiput not too pronounced

EARS high set, clipped to point, fairly long, shell not too broad; carried erect

NECK round, length ample; strong, muscular, clean; no dewlap; distinctly marked nape, elegant arch

SHOULDERS long, sloping, close-lying; not too muscular

BACK short, straight, broad, muscular; withers clearly defined; loins short, muscular. Croup slightly sloped, broad

ELBOWS not too close, yet not off too far

PASTERNS clearly defined, short; slight slant but almost perpendicular to ground

RIBS well-arched, extending far to rear

UNDERLINE graceful curve

TAIL—set-high rather than too deep; clipped; carried upward

PELVIS long; broad in females

THIGHS broad, curved; breech musculation strongly developed; long

HINDQUARTER JOINTS well-angulated; in balance with forequarters; thighs broad, curved; breech musculation strongly developed

HIND LEGS straight, viewed from rear; hocks clean, not distended; hock joints perpendicular to ground

FEET strong pads; rear toes slightly longer than front, catlike

COLOR fawn, in various shades from light yellow to dark deer red; brindle should have black stripes on fawn background; stripes clearly defined, covering top of body; while marking not rejected

DISQUALIFICATIONS—white or black ground color, or entirely white or black or any color other than fawn or brindle. (White markings allowed but must not exceed one-third of ground color)

[67]

HOW A DOG BECOMES
AN OBEDIENCE CHAMPION

Obedience degrees appear *after* the dog's name.

C.D. means *Companion Dog*
C.D.X. means *Companion Dog Excellent*
U.D. means *Utility Dog*
U.D.T. means *Utility Dog Tracker*
T.D. means *Tracking Dog*
T.D.X. means *Tracking Dog Excellent*

In the obedience classes, all breeds compete against one another. There are three classes, Novice, Open and Utility. There is also a Tracking Test, but this is not held at a dog show.

In order to win obedience degrees, a dog must receive a certain score; he must pass under different judges, and he must compete against other dogs. The exciting thing about obedience trials is that a dog that fails one day can win top honors the next.

An Obedience Trial Champion title (O.T. Ch.) appears *before* the dog's name. Only dogs that have earned the Utility Dog title are eligible to earn points toward the 100 points, which together with three specified First Place wins under three different judges, are required for an Obedience Trial Championship.

REQUIREMENTS FOR THE
NOVICE CLASS (C.D. DEGREE)

Heel on Leash & Figure Eight .... 40 Points
Stand for Examination .... 30 Points
Heel Free .... 40 Points
Recall .... 30 Points
Long Sit .... 30 Points
Long Down .... 30 Points

Maximum Total Score .... 200 Points

(Less Penalty for Misbehavior)

REQUIREMENTS FOR THE
OPEN CLASS (C.D.X. DEGREE)

Heel Free .... 40 Points
Drop on Recall .... 30 Points
Retrieve on Flat .... 20 Points
Retrieve over High Jump .... 30 Points
Broad Jump .... 20 Points
Long Sit .... 30 Points
Long Down .... 30 Points

Maximum Total Score .... 200 Points

(Less Penalty for Misbehavior)

REQUIREMENTS FOR
UTILITY CLASS

Signal Exercise	40 Points
Scent Discrimination	
Article No. 1	30 Points
Scent Discrimination	
Article No. 2	30 Points
Directed Retrieve	30 Points
Directed Jumping	40 Points
Group Examination	30 Points
Maximum Total Score	200 Points

(Less Penalty for Misbehavior)

T.D. (TRACKING DOG)

The Tracking Test, held separately from a dog show, requires the dog to follow the scent of a stranger for 440 to 500 yards on a track that is one-half to two hours old. A Tracking Dog should be able to find a criminal or a lost person.

T.D.X. (TRACKING DOG EXCELLENT)

The Tracking Dog Excellent Test requires the dog to follow the scent of a stranger for 800 to 1,000 yards on a track that is three to four hours old, and which has been crossed at two widely separated places by more recent tracks.

[70]

DOG SHOW RULES

Your dog must be over six months of age before you can enter him in a licensed dog show.

He must be pure-bred.

He must be registered or eligible for registration with the American Kennel Club.

He must have no disqualifying faults such as blindness, lameness or other faults set up by the Standard for the breed.

Your dog can't be dyed or have his color changed in any way.

Once you take your dog on the show ground, you must show him in all classes in which he is entered.

In obedience, your dog must work accurately, and you must handle him with care.

There are other rules pertaining to color, physical make-up, size, and temperament in obedience. Make certain you are familiar with all the rules before you enter your dog in a breed show or an obedience trial. Otherwise you may be told that your dog has been disqualified or that he does not pass in obedience.

Dog shows are run by Superintendents licensed by the American Kennel Club. Premium lists, mailed in advance, advertise the shows and tell who the judges will be. Money and trophies make up the awards. Kennel owners, veterinarians, or other people who work with dogs can tell you how to get your name on a mailing list so you will know when and where a dog show will be held.

Send for this booklet if you want to show your dog in a breed show.

Send for this booklet if you want to show your dog in obedience trials. Both are available from the American Kennel Club, 51 Madison Avenue, New York, N.Y. 10010. In Canada, the Canadian Kennel Club, 2150 Bloor Street, W., Toronto, Ontario, Canada M6S-4V7.

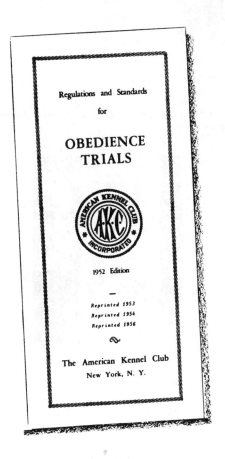

DOG SHOW RIBBONS

1st	2nd	3rd	4th	Winners
(Blue)	(Red)	(Yellow)	(White)	(Purple)

Note: The only ribbon that awards points toward a dog's championship, is the purple one.

Reserve Winners

(Purple & White)

Best of Winners

(Blue & White)

Best of Breed or Best of Variety (Purple & Gold)

Best of Opposite Sex

(Red & White)

[74]

SANCTIONED MATCHES

Watch for these to come in your town. A sanctioned match is a show where, at little expense, one can find out if his dog is good enough to compete in a regular show or if he has had enough training to enter an obedience trial. A sanctioned match is run like a regular show, but wins do not count toward the dog's championship or toward his obedience degrees.

JUNIOR SHOWMANSHIP CLASSES

Junior Showmanship Classes are for young people. Different age groups from ten to sixteen compete for ribbons and prizes at almost every dog show. The awards are based on how well boys and girls show their dogs in the breed ring. This doesn't mean, however, that a young person can't exhibit his dog in a regular breed class or obedience trial where it is the dog that counts.

Taking your dog with you on vacation this year? Prepare him now!

Train your dog to do his duties while on leash. Tell him, "Duties! Duties!" so he will hurry things up. If he is modest and slow to learn, fasten two leashes together or use a long rope.

Take your dog in the car as often as you can before you leave on vacation so he will learn to ride without getting sick.

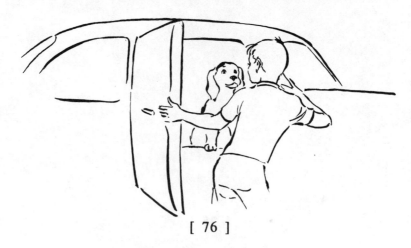

Make him behave in the car. Tie him or threaten him with a small rolled magazine if he acts wild.

Make him wait for permission to leave the car.

Touring with Towser, distributed by the Gaines Dog Research Center, 250 North St., White Plains, N.Y. 10625, lists the hotels and motels all over the country that take dogs. There is a mailing fee for the booklet, but it is very useful.

Fasten your dog's license and rabies tags to his collar.

Carry a health certificate from your veterinarian.

In case your dog gets lost, hang another tag on his collar, giving your home address.

And REMEMBER! When you leave your dog in the car, it must be parked in the shade with windows partly open for air.

Here are some things the traveler may need; take as many as you can:

A collar and leash
A long line for exercise
A supply of dog food
A can opener
A mixing spoon
A feeding pan
A water thermos
Brush and comb
One or two towels
Your dog's blanket
Newspapers
A thermometer, in case you need to take your dog's temperature
Glycerine suppositories (to make him go to the bathroom)
Something for diarrhea
And, if there is room, a small dog crate or folding wire cage

If you are traveling by air, rail or sea, call the transportation authorities. Rules vary. For instance, you can rent a crate from certain air lines. With others, you have to furnish your own. And never, *never* attempt to ship a dog anywhere without a health certificate, and rabies shot if the country or state requires one.

DOG TIPS

A dog whose ancestry is known to consist of many generations of the same breed, with no mixture of blood from any other breeds, is a *pure-bred*. Don't call your dog a "thorough-bred."

A "police" dog is a dog that does police work, such as guarding or sentry duty. This is not another name for the German Shepherd dog, or any other breed.

A "registered" dog is a dog that is on record at the American Kennel Club. One eligible for registration has not been registered himself but his parents have.

Even though a dog has been inoculated against distemper and hepatitis, he can still catch these diseases. Remember to give your dog a booster shot once a year. When your dog gets old, limit stairs. Give him a warm place to sleep, and overlook his grouchiness. A regular physical examination will tell you if your dog needs a special diet, and through your kind words and loving pats, he will know you still love him in his old age.

DOG SENSE

Never reach to pat a dog you don't know. If a dog wants to be friendly, he will come to you.

Never run or scream when a dog growls or barks at you; stand still. In a low, demanding voice, say, "Go home!" or "Scat!" When you move on, continue slowly.

Never reach for a frightened dog. Using the leash or a piece of rope, make a noose and drop it slowly over the dog's head. If he is a small dog and you want to pick him up, pull the leash forward and hold it tight. Lift him by reaching under his hindquarters.

SOME INTERESTING FACTS

Do you know:

Silver Poodles are born black.

Dalmatians are born white and spots appear later.

Greyhounds can run as fast as 45 miles an hour.

The Basenji doesn't bark; he chortles.

This is called "pointing," a dog's way of saying, "Something is hiding in those bushes."

Working dogs were bred to perform a special service.

Borzoi is another name for the Russian Wolfhound.

Schipperke, in Flemish, means "little Captain."

THESE ARE THE PROPER NAMES FOR THE PARTS OF YOUR DOG'S BODY

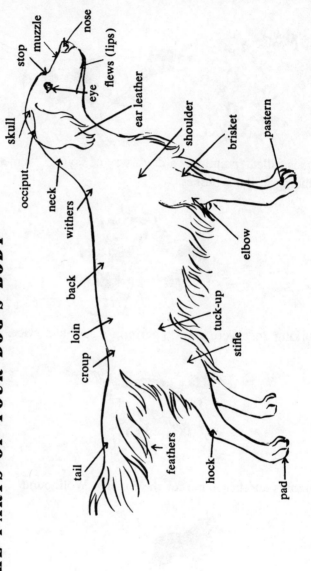

DOG PROFESSIONS—

If you want to work with dogs when you grow up:

Dog Artist	Kennel Assistant
Dog Beautician	Kennel Manager
Dog Breeder	Manager of a boarding kennel
Dog Broker (one who imports and exports dogs)	Pet Shop Owner
Dog Food Salesman	Professional Handler
Dog Judge	Professional Trainer
Dog Photographer	Superintendent of Dog Shows
Dog Sitter (for city dogs)	Supplier of Dog Accessories
Dog Walker (service for city dogs)	Training Class Instructor
Dog Writer	Veterinarian
Humane Society Worker	Veterinarian's Assistant

DOG DIARY

Breed _____

Name _____

Color and markings _____

Sex _____

Birthday   _____   _____   _____
                day   month   year

State License number _____

American Kennel Club number (if registered) _____

Where purchased _____

Date of purchase _____

PHOTOGRAPH

PEDIGREE

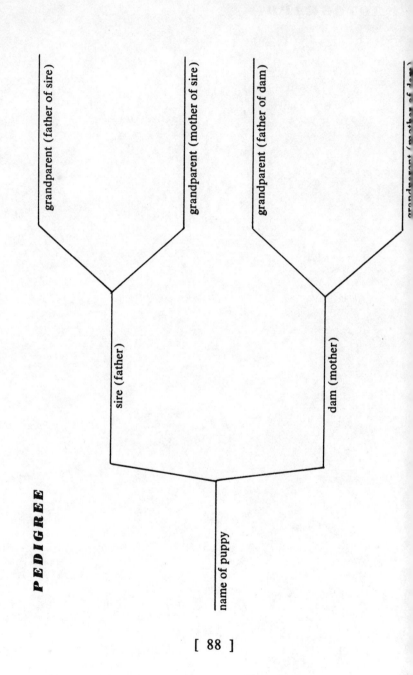

name of puppy

sire (father)

dam (mother)

grandparent (father of sire)

grandparent (mother of sire)

grandparent (father of dam)

grandparent (mother of dam)

SHOTS

Distemper

_____   _____
date   Veterinarian

_____   _____
date   Veterinarian

Hepatitis

_____   _____
date   Veterinarian

_____   _____
date   Veterinarian

Booster

_____   _____
date   Veterinarian

_____   _____
date   Veterinarian

_____   _____
date   Veterinarian

Rabies

_____   _____
date   Veterinarian

_____   _____
date   Veterinarian

Worming

_____   _____
date   Kind

_____   _____
date   Kind

Important dates to remember (if female)

When in season 1_____

2_____

3_____

4_____

5_____

6_____

Important telephone numbers

Local Veterinarian _____

Local Police _____

Local S.P.C.A. _____

SHOW RECORD

OBEDIENCE RECORD

AGE RECORD

Dogs age faster than humans do. You can roughly judge how old your dog is in comparison to man by the table below:

Dog's Age	Man's Age
6 Months	10 Years
8 Months	13 Years
10 Months	14 Years
12 Months	15 Years
18 Months	20 Years
2 Years	24 Years
4 Years	32 Years
6 Years	40 Years
8 Years	48 Years
10 Years	56 Years
12 Years	64 Years
14 Years	72 Years
16 Years	80 Years
18 Years	88 Years
20 Years	96 Years
21 Years	100 Years

WHAT YOU SHOULD KNOW IN BUYING A REGISTERED DOG:

When you buy a dog that is represented as being eligible for registration with The American Kennel Club, you are entitled to receive an AKC application form properly filled out by the seller, which—when completed by you and submitted to the AKC with the proper fee—will enable you to effect the registration of the dog. When the application has been processed, you will receive an AKC registration certificate.

Under AKC rules, any person who sells dogs that are represented as being AKC registrable, must maintain records that will make it possible to give full identifying information with every dog delivered, even though AKC papers may not yet be available. *Do not accept a promise of later identification.*

The Rules and Regulations of The American Kennel Club stipulate that whenever someone sells or delivers a dog that is said to be registrable with the AKC, the dog must be identified either by putting into the hands of the buyer a properly completed AKC registration application, or by giving the buyer a bill of sale or a written statement, *signed by the seller,* giving the dog's full breeding information as follows:
   —**Breed, sex and color of the dog**
   —**Date of birth of the dog**
   —**Registered names of the dog's sire and dam**
   —**Name of the breeder**

If you encounter any problems in acquiring the necessary registration application forms, it is suggested that you write The

American Kennel Club, 51 Madison Avenue, New York, N.Y. 10010, *giving full particulars* and the difficulty will be reviewed. All individuals acquiring a dog represented as being AKC registrable should realize it is their responsibility to obtain complete identification of the dog as described above sufficient to identify in AKC records, or THEY SHOULD NOT BUY THE DOG.

BOOK TWO

DOG TRAINING
for Boys and Girls

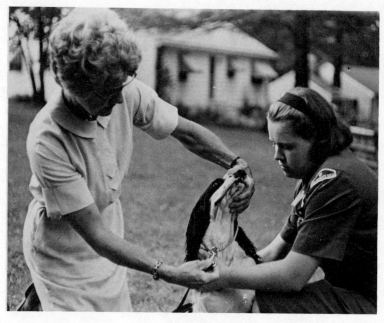

No one has done more to develop American interest in dog training than did Blanche Saunders. The pioneer (together with Mrs. Whitehouse Walker) of Obedience training in this country, virtually every waking moment of her adult life was spent in its promotion. Miss Saunders took especial delight in teaching boys and girls to train their dogs. Here, in one of the last pictures made before her death of a heart attack in December 1964, she is shown demonstrating to a Girl Scout the proper method of putting on a choke chain collar.

CONTENTS for BOOK TWO
DOG TRAINING for BOYS and GIRLS

TO PARENTS, TEACHERS AND LIBRARIANS

Children and dogs go together like candy and cake. Doctors and psychologists urge parents to get a dog for wholesome contribution to the mental and physical growing-up processes of their children.

This book solves the problem parents face when, after the first thrill of dog ownership, the children lose interest in training the family pet. In simple words and exact drawings, the author and artist make dog training a longlasting joy to the girl or boy. The effect on the young trainer's character, confidence and sense of accomplishment—not to mention the dog's acceptance by family, friends and neighbors—cannot be measured.

PART 1

YOUR PUPPY'S
EARLY TRAINING

THE NEW PUPPY

Never give a puppy the run of the house. If you don't have a playpen or a wire cage, keep the puppy in the bathroom or kitchen with a gate across the door. Put papers on the floor. Take away things a puppy might chew (like rugs and chairs) and give him a toy to play with. (He will love one made of rawhide.) Look in often and if he is being good, tell him **"Good boy!"**

STAYING ALONE

Most kennel owners will tell you, "The first thing your puppy must learn is to stay alone so he won't bark when you leave him." Staying alone also teaches a puppy not to chew or wet in spite.

Give your puppy a clock that ticks loudly, a hot water bottle to cuddle against, or leave a radio playing, but don't go to him when he yells. Puppies like to have you come back to them even if it means a spanking. Instead, toss a magazine or a small pan at the door and say **"Quiet!"** Do this every time your puppy makes a fuss and he will soon learn to stay alone quietly.

PAPER-BREAKING

Train your puppy to go to the bathroom on papers so he can have more freedom. When he selects one corner of the room for his duties, take up the other papers, a few at a time. If he misses the paper, shame him. If he does what he should on them, praise him and tell him he is a good puppy. Your puppy will soon learn what the papers are for.

After you have trained your puppy to use papers, put papers on the floor in the room where he sleeps. Place him on papers and hold him there with the leash, immediately after he eats. Put him on papers after he wakes from a nap or after an exciting game. Tell him **"Duties! Duties!"** When he does what he should, praise him and tell him he is a g-o-o-o-d boy.

HOUSE MANNERS

House rules include:

    Little barking
    No chewing
    No stealing
    Stay alone quietly
    Stay off furniture
    No jumping on people
    Be clean in the house.

Your puppy will more quickly learn the difference between right and wrong:

    If you are patient.
    If you are watchful and prevent mistakes.
    If you correct when mistakes are made.
    If you correct *every time* a mistake is made.

For example: If you want your puppy to stay off the furniture, push him down every time he gets up. If he sneaks up when you aren't there, place something in his favorite chair that will jump or make a squawking noise. A wound-up toy should do the trick.

THE WORD "NO"

If your puppy barks more than he should, cuff his nose gently and tell him **"NO!"**

If he uses the table leg for a bone or thinks the cookies in the dish belong to him, again tap his nose and tell him **"NO!"** Use this word every time your puppy does wrong.

If the puppy is where you can't reach him, throw a magazine near him. A puppy learns right from wrong by associating his act with pleasing or displeasing results.

JUMPING ON PEOPLE

Does your puppy jump on you? The next time he comes running, spread your fingers fan-like and say **"No jumping!"** If he jumps up in spite of the warning, bump his nose once with the palm of your hand. Tell him **"Sit!"** Then pat him.

If you are training a big dog, lift your knee and bump his chest. A tumble backward should teach him to keep his paws on the ground. After you bump him, pat him or his feelings will be hurt.

HOUSE-BREAKING

When your puppy is three or four months old, it is time to house-break him. Pick up the papers. From now on, he must go to the bathroom outdoors.

These rules help to house-break a puppy:

Don't let the puppy run loose in the house unless he has done everything outside.

Take the puppy outdoors when he wakes in the morning.

Take him outdoors the last thing at night.

Take him out after he eats, after he plays and when he wakes up from a nap.

Praise him when he does what he should outdoors.

MORE ABOUT HOUSE-BREAKING

When your puppy is free in the house, you must be there to watch him. When he sniffs the floor and runs around excitedly, hurry! Take him outdoors. For the first few times you give the puppy the run of the house, take him out after the first fifteen minutes and then every hour.

At night, tie the puppy where you can hear him if he asks to go out, or put him in a crate or a wire cage so he can't wander. When a puppy roams, he is apt to wet.

When your puppy makes a mistake in the house, take him by the collar and show him where he did wrong. Shame him and then shake him. If you did not catch him in the act, don't be too angry with him.

If your puppy wets or messes in front of you, you can be more strict. Toss something, like his leash or a small magazine, and startle him. Call him and pat him.

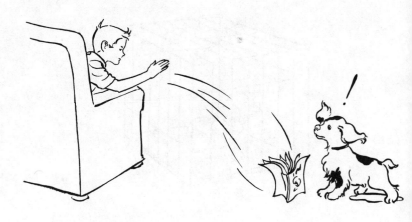

Every puppy should be trained to go to the bathroom on leash. If your puppy won't cooperate, tie him where you can watch him or put him in a crate until it is time for his next outing.

When you take your puppy out for exercise:

Fasten two leashes together to give him more freedom.

Take him where other dogs have been.

Keep telling him **"Duties! Duties!"**

When he does what he should, praise him and pat him. Let him know you are pleased.

LEASH TRAINING

When you take your puppy for a walk, fasten the collar tight enough so it can't slip over his head. Kneel, and coax him to take a few steps. Then he won't be afraid. If he sits down or pulls away from you, start walking fast and call his name. Soon he will follow you.

STAIRS

After you train your puppy to walk on leash, teach him to go up and down stairs. Carry him the first few steps. Then coax him. If he draws back, pull slowly on the leash and keep telling him **"Good Boy! Good Boy!"** After he staggers up or down the first few steps, the others will be easy.

WALKING WITH THE LEASH

When you take your puppy for a walk, put the handle of the leash around your wrist like this:

Puppies are sometimes frightened and they jump unexpectedly. With the handle around your wrist, the leash can't slip through your fingers.

When you see a car coming, or whenever you hear the toot of a horn, pull the puppy quickly off to the side of the road. Do this regularly and your dog will move to safety by himself when a motor car approaches.

HONK! HONK!

THE OWNER

Here are other things you should learn:

When you want your puppy to come, kneel. Then reach for him slowly and pick him up gently. Grabbing makes a dog duck away.

Never call your puppy and then spank him. If he needs a scolding, go to him, hold his collar and tell him he was bad.

Never yell at your dog! Dogs' ears are sensitive. Use a stern tone and you will get better results.

Never pull things from your dog or play tug-of-war. This teaches a dog to bite.

Never tease your puppy. It will make him cross.

And when you praise your puppy, put praise in your voice.

Be patient. Make sure your puppy knows each lesson well before you teach him the next lesson. Practice with him often, but do not tire him out.

PART 2

OBEDIENCE TRAINING

SIMPLE TRAINING

Simple commands of **"Come,"** **"Sit,"** and **"Lie down"** should be taught at three to four months of age. Your puppy will learn very quickly to come when he is called if every time he answers the call, he receives a pleasant reward such as a piece of meat, dog candy, or a word of praise.

He will quickly learn the command **"Sit"** if his head is held high and a little pressure is applied to his hindquarters. He will learn the meaning of **"Lie Down"** if you press on his shoulders and pull down on his collar. When you do these things, keep telling the puppy that he is a **"Good Boy."**

The young puppy should learn not to pull on the leash. Use an ordinary leather collar for this training and tug gently on the leash until the puppy learns not to pull ahead.

OBEDIENCE TRAINING

When you train your dog obedience at six months, you need a chain slip collar for the big strong dog.

A chain leather one or a nylon slip collar for the small dog or the puppy.

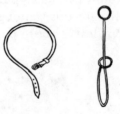

You need a leash a foot longer than you are tall. Get one with a strong snap. The pinch kind may open by accident. Get a leash made of flat leather. A round one or a chain leash will hurt your hands.

LEARN HOW TO PUT ON
THE COLLAR

If you are right-handed and your dog walks at your left, the correct collar looks like this.

This is wrong.

If you are left-handed and your dog walks on your right, the collar is reversed.

(Right)

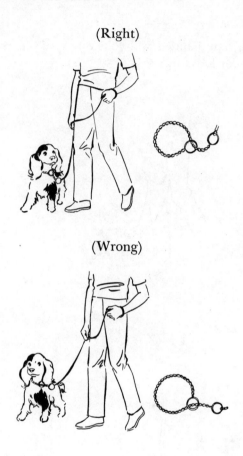

(Wrong)

For the purpose of teaching, we will assume that your dog walks on your left.

HOW TO HOLD THE LEASH

Take the leash in BOTH hands. Hold your hands close to
your body and keep your left elbow straight.

KNOW YOUR DOG'S
TEMPERAMENT

Handle the shy dog gently. Gain his confidence through encouragement and praise.

Pep up the lazy worker. Move quickly yourself and your dog will move quickly.

If your dog is a clown, speak more sharply and correct with firmness.

If he is stubborn, make each correction more severe.

While training, keep your dog's attention. When he looks away, nudge him with your knee.

When he sniffs the ground, give the leash a tug.

For all corrections, snap the leash!

Never drag on it.

For best results, praise your dog when you give him a command. Praise him when you use the leash.

HEELING

Heeling means to walk at your side without pulling. Every time your dog passes your knee, say **"Heel,"** jerk the leash backward, and pat your side to encourage him to stay close.

If he passes your knee a second time, stand still and jerk the leash harder!

If your dog holds back instead, *don't* jerk the leash. Pull on it gently and keep saying **"Good Boy! Good Boy!"** After he takes a few steps, slacken the leash and pat your side.

While training, stand up straight and don't slow up when you turn!

Don't let your dog play with the leash.

Don't let him climb on you.

Before long your dog will understand that if he runs ahead or darts off to the side, he will hear the word **"Heel!"** and feel a sharp tug on his collar. If he stays close to your knee, praise him and pat him.

SITTING

To make your dog sit, shorten the leash in your right hand and pull up. Say "**Sit!**" and push on his hindquarters with your left hand. Dogs like to be praised, so while you make him sit, tell him he is a good boy.

If he braces himself, spank him once on his rear and tell him more firmly "**SIT!**" Now pat him with the same hand you spanked him with so he will think you spanked him in play. At the same time, push his hips over. Make him sit straight!!

When you tell your dog "**Sit!**," don't step toward him or he will jump away.

Don't let him use you as a leaning post. Bump him with your knee!

If he sits too far away, coax him to sit close.

If he sits ahead, pull him backward.

The proper sit is even with your knee, square and facing straight ahead.

When you take your dog on the street, make him walk at heel. Practice making him sit. Your dog should obey wherever he is.

STAYING

When you want your dog to stay, hold your left hand in front of his face, tell him **"Stay!"** and step forward on your right foot.

When you turn to face him, turn your hand so the palm is toward the dog.

If he starts forward, bump him once under the chin to remind him you said **"Stay!"**

For some dogs, learning to stay is a very hard lesson. If your
dog thinks you are playing games, speak more sharply!

If he stands, "spank" him to a sitting position.

If he is lazy, use your leash.

Your dog may even try to run away.

Most of all, don't keep telling your dog "**Stay! Stay! Stay!**" if he is staying. Wait until he moves before you tell him again.

RETURN TO HEEL POSITION

When you circle your dog, walk close to him and hold the leash to your left. Your dog can turn his head but don't let him turn his body.

If he tries to get up when you walk in back of him, hold him and keep him sitting.

And remember the pat and praise when you give him permission to move.

Test your dog but stand on the leash in case he tries to dart away.

Make him stay while you put on your hat and coat to take him for a walk.

Make him stay while you fix his dinner.

And while you pack the car for a picnic.

Tell him **"Stay!"** so he won't dash out an open door.

With practice, he will even learn to stay when the telephone rings.

COMING WHEN CALLED

When a puppy is small, we kneel; we coax; we bribe with food to get him to come. Now that your dog is growing up, teach him to come because you called him.

Put him on leash and when he is busy sniffing the ground or saying ugly things to another dog, call his name and tell him **"Come!"** After you call, jerk ONCE on the leash with lots of praise.

OSCAR, COME!

Your dog will come gaily if you clap your hands and make a game of the training.

He will learn more quickly if you give the command before you jerk the leash, and make a fuss over him after he comes.

GOOD BOY!

Leave the dog in a sitting position. Then stand behind him. Call him! If he doesn't move, tug once on the leash and give him extra praise.

OSCAR, COME!

When he is off leash, ask a friend or one of your family to help. When you call your dog, ask the friend to point to you and tell the dog **"Go!"** The friend should even chase him if necessary. Your dog will quickly learn that if he goes to the person who calls, he will be praised and patted. If he goes somewhere else, people will chase after him and tell him **"Go! Go!"**

If there is no one to chase your dog, turn and walk away.
Perhaps he will follow.

If he plays hard-to-get, make him curious!

Never, NEVER grab!

Reach for him slowly. Pick up a small dog gently by support-ing his chest with one hand while he sits on the other arm.

A dog biscuit or a piece of dog candy will also help teach your dog to come.

LYING DOWN

If you move slowly and give lots of praise, your dog will not struggle when you make him lie down. Hold the leash in both hands. Let the center of the leash rest on the floor. Step over the leash with your right foot so it will slide in front of your heel, and tell your dog **"Stay!"**

Now that you are ready, quietly say **"Lie Down!"** Then keep repeating **"Good Boy! Good Boy!"** while you pull *slowly* on the leash.

If you are training a small dog, reach with your right hand and press gently on the shoulders. While you push him to the floor, scratch his back and give praise.

If your dog braces himself, don't force him! Stay just as you are and wait for him to relax. When he does, pull up slowly on the leash with continuous praise.

If your small dog gets excited, stand on the leash, and use both hands to draw his front paws gently toward you. While you do it, give praise.

After your dog goes down, tell him **"Good Boy!"** and scratch his ear.

When you teach your dog to lie down at your side, use your left hand to pull down on the leash. If he lifts his head or tries to nip, turn your face away and hold tight. When you hold, keep whispering **"Good Boy! Good Boy!"** so he will relax.

Small dogs feel more secure when you use BOTH hands to make them lie down. Pull down on the leash with the left hand and press on the dog's shoulders with your right hand. If you give continuous praise, your dog should go down without trouble.

DOWN
GOOD BOY!

When your dog will lie down on command, teach him to obey a signal. Tell him **"Stay!"** Face him. Hold your right hand in a salute with fingers pointing up. Then tell him **"Lie Down!"** After you give the command, slide the leash under your right foot by pulling up with the left hand. Keep your right hand raised until your dog goes down.

Practice making your dog lie down in strange places. Make him lie down when he is excited. He probably will not stay but keep at him until he does. If he gets up without permission, put him down quickly and tell him **"Stay!"** with more authority. When he has stayed down for one or two minutes, release him. Praise him and give him a big pat.

STANDING

Your dog's obedience lessons now consist of heeling, sitting, staying, lying down and coming when called. He must also learn to stand and to remain standing.

Wad the leash into a ball and hold it in your right hand. Now place your hand that holds the leash in front of your dog's face and reach over his back with your left hand so you can rub his stomach. Tell him **"Stand!"** and pull the leash forward.

Your dog will learn to stand at heel instead of sitting if, while walking, you place your right hand in front of his face and tell him "Stand!" At the same time, scratch his back with your left hand and give him lots of praise.

If he starts walking ahead, bump his nose with the hand that holds the leash. After you bump him, pat him on the nose and tell him he is a good dog so his feelings will not be hurt.

Train your small dog by looping the handle of the leash under his stomach. Tell him **"Stand!"** and if he tries to sit, lift him very gently to a standing position.

To keep your dog standing, place your left hand in front of his muzzle. Tell him **"Stay!"** and step forward on your right foot, just as you did when you left your dog sitting.

When you turn to face him, turn your head also.

If your dog creeps toward you, a cuff under his chin will remind him you said "Stay!"

When sitting is your problem, tap him lightly under his stomach.

If your dog still will not stand, straddle him over a broom handle placed on the rungs of two chairs. If your dog is small, place an empty coffee can under him.

STAY!

Never pull your dog's tail to make him stand!

Or his skin.

Lift him gently by tickling his stomach.

Return to heel position by circling your dog just as you did in the sit-stay.

With practice, your dog will learn to stand without moving away, even when someone touches him.

GRADUATION

Graduation comes nine weeks after you start training. Here is what your dog must do in order to win a dog school diploma with his name on it:

> He must walk and make turns without pulling on the leash. When you come to a halt, he must sit without being told.

> He must lie down when you tell him and come when he is called.

> He must remain standing while a stranger touches him on the head, back and tail.

> He must stay sitting for one minute without a second command.

> He must lie down for three minutes.

HAPPY TRAINING!

PART 3

TRICKS FOR
YOUR DOG

TRICKS

"BEG"

Put your dog on leash and tell him to **"Sit!"** Then hold a piece of meat or dog candy above his head. Encourage him with **"Beg! Beg!"** When he lifts his paws from the floor, praise him and give him the tid-bit. If he stands on his back legs, take the food away, tell him to sit and then start over again.

Or, hold your dog in a sitting-up position by lifting both paws until he learns to balance on his haunches.

"SHAKE"

Make your dog sit. Then hold out your hand. When you say **"Shake"** or **"Give paw!"** tap the heel of one paw lightly. At the same time, push him slightly off balance with your other hand. While you hold his paw, give him his reward.

"PLAY POSSUM"

Make your dog lie on his side. Then soothe him by stroking him gently. Keep repeating **"Play Possum, Stay!"** When he relaxes, take your hands away. Release him by saying **"O.K.!"**

"ROLL OVER"

After your dog learns **"Play Possum!"** teach him **"Roll Over!"** Put him on his side. Then take hold of the front and back paws on the underside of his body. Say **"Roll Over!"** Then quickly flip him over. When he jumps to his feet, praise him and pat him. The circle motion used to flip your dog over later becomes the signal for this trick.

"CATCH"

Use a soft ball and throw it into the air. A hard ball thrown with force directly at your dog might break a tooth. When you throw the ball say **"Catch!"** It may bounce off his nose a few times but he will soon learn to grab for it when he sees it coming.

"JUMP!"

Buy a play hoop or make one out of wire. Put your dog on leash, slip the leash through the center of the hoop, say **"Jump!"** and pull him through. Hold the hoop low and say **"Jump!"** before you pull on the leash, so your dog will learn to jump on command.

"CARRY!"

Carefully place a small object, like an old glove, a leather wallet or the handle of a small basket, in your dog's mouth and flatter him with "Aren't you smart!" Scratching his back will also help teach your dog to carry.

"OUT!"

Never take things from your dog by pulling. When you want him to let go, take hold of the object with one hand and say "Out!" If he won't give it up, surprise him with a little cuff on the nose with the free hand. When he drops what he is holding, praise him and pat him.

"DANCE!"

Hold something to eat above your dog's head and teach him to dance. When he stands on his back legs to reach the food, say "Dance!" and move your hand in a circle to make the dog pivot. After he turns, give him the food and praise him.

"PRAYERS"

Make your dog sit in front of a low bench. Place his front paws on the bench. Say **"Prayers!"** and gently push his head down. At the same time, offer him food between his front legs. Release him with **"Amen!"** or **"O.K.!"**

"WAIT!"

Place a ball or a piece of dog biscuit on your dog's nose between his eyes. Tell him **"Wait!"** After a moment or two tell him **"O.K.!"** and see if he can catch it. This trick may take a lot of practice.

"TAKE A BOW!"

Take advantage of your dog's natural ways to teach additional tricks. When he stretches, say **"Take a bow!"**

"SPEAK!"

When he barks or sniffles, put your finger in the air and say **"Speak!"** or **"Sneeze!"** It won't take long for your dog to learn that whenever he makes a noise he will get a reward.

SHOWING YOUR DOG

If you own a pure-bred dog, registered in the American Kennel Club or Canadian Kennel Club, you may like to show him or enter him in Obedience Classes.

A dog club may hold dog shows or run Obedience training classes in your home town or nearby. You can ask the kennel where you bought your dog or your local veterinarian for dog clubs near you and the names and addresses of their secretaries. A club secretary can tell you where you can learn to train your dog for showing and obedience.

Humane societies, like the ASPCA, often conduct training classes in Obedience. You can take a dog of mixed-breed to these classes.

You will enjoy taking your dog, if he is well-trained, to pet shows run by schools or young people's groups like the Scouts.

PART 4

THE PROBLEM DOG

THE DOG THAT RUNS AWAY

If your dog runs away when he knows the meaning of the word **come**, the next time you go for a walk, carry a rolled magazine. If he does not listen when you call him, throw the magazine at his heels, kneel, call him again and praise him while he is coming to you.

THE CAT CHASER

The next time you take your dog where there is a cat, carry a small rolled magazine. Put your dog on leash and introduce him to the cat. Hold the rolled magazine and if he lunges forward say **"NO!"** and quickly lower the magazine between them. If he is off leash and makes a dash for the cat, throw what you are holding at the dog's heels and tell him firmly **"COME!"**

THE CAR CHASER

Break the habit of chasing cars by arming yourself with two or three empty food cans and one or two empty cartons. Hide in the car while someone else drives. When your dog comes running out, and the car has stopped, jump out and chase him by throwing things at him.

THE PLAYFUL BITER

When a puppy nips in play, biting is apt to become a habit. When your puppy grabs at your arm or at your clothing, cuff him on the nose and tell him **"NO!"** After you cuff him, pat him. This annoying habit could make your parents dispose of your dog.

THE SERIOUS BITER

Dogs bite for three reasons: to guard, when they don't want to do something, and when they are afraid.

Scold the over-protective dog. Make him understand that he must never attack because he feels like guarding.

Muzzle the fear-biter. Force him in a kind way to let strangers handle him. In time he may get over being frightened.

If your dog resents combing or growls when you take his bone away, rap him sharply on the tip of the nose and tell him you will have none of that! Don't bully him but let him know you are the master.

THE CHEWER

Confine the dog that chews in a room where he can do little damage. Give him toys and bones made of hard rubber or rawhide, or give him a tennis ball. Wait until you catch him chewing on something he shouldn't, then startle him! Throw something at the spot and tell him **"NO!"** Throw the object when he isn't looking at you.

THE DIGGER

You may not be able to stop your dog completely from digging but you can discourage the habit. The next time you see him uprooting the flower bed or digging holes in the lawn, toss something at the spot and call out **"NO!"** Do this every time he starts to dig.

THE DOG THAT WETS
IN SPITE

If your dog wets to "get even," have someone hide where the dog can't see him. Play with another dog or go away and leave him. If out of jealousy or resentfulness he leaves a "spite" puddle, the person hiding can throw something or scold him and catch him in the act.

THE THIEF

Does your dog steal things from your closet? Balance a small pie pan on the inside handle of the slightly open door. Your dog will make the correction himself when the pan falls.

THE CAVE MAN

Does your dog hide under the chair or the bed and growl when you try to get him out? Ask someone to drive him out by poking at him so he will run to you for protection. When he does, reward him with a pat.

THE DOG THAT WILL NOT
STAY ALONE

Put your dog in a room by himself *while you or some member of the family are at home* to make the necessary correction. Every time the dog barks or scratches to get out, bang on the door or throw a small pie pan so it lands with a crash. In ten or fifteen minutes, if he has been quiet, let him out. Don't make the mistake of keeping your dog with you all the time. Teach him independence!

When a dog will stay alone, owners avoid the problems of barking, chewing and wetting out of spite.

THE DOG THAT ROAMS

Don't let your dog get into the habit of roaming. Call him back every time he leaves the property. If this doesn't work, ask your friends and family to help. Let them stand outside an open gate or at the end of the driveway and when your dog starts to leave, have them block him by tossing an empty carton in front of him. At the same time they should tell him **"Home!"**

THE DOG THAT WILL NOT
GET INTO A CAR

Put the leash on and have the dog's collar tight enough so it cannot slip over his head. Get into the car yourself. Then use a steady pull and give constant praise. After your dog climbs in, pat him.

PART 5

MAKING FRIENDS
FOR YOUR DOG

HOW TO MAKE FRIENDS
FOR YOUR DOG

When you take your dog visiting, keep him on leash. He may be clean at home but he will be tempted to misbehave in strange places.

Don't let your male dog lift his leg on shrubbery or evergreen trees. Exercise your female where there is long grass. The acid in dog urine kills growing plants.

When you take your dog on the street, if he barks at people or other dogs, cuff his nose or give him a shaking. Tell him "No!" Don't let him dirty sidewalks or run wildly at the end of the leash.

When you take your puppy riding, car rules are the same as for young people:

No climbing back and forth from one seat to another.

No hanging out the windows.

Little noise.

If the dog will not stay put, tie him or hold the leash so he cannot jump around.

For the dog that barks at people or dogs when he is in the car, carry a fly swatter or a small rolled magazine and threaten him. He will know what it's for!

When you travel with your dog, keep him off hotel and motel beds unless you cover the bed with his blanket. Don't use towels and washcloths to clean up after your dog. Don't feed him without first putting down newspapers.

If you have not trained your dog to stay alone, don't leave him by himself where there are close neighbors.

Keep your dog off taxi seats and public benches.

Obey the "No dogs allowed" signs.

Follow these rules and your dog will make friends wherever he goes.